HIGHLIGHTS OF ADB'S COOPERATION WITH CIVIL SOCIETY ORGANIZATIONS 2020

APRIL 2021

ADB

ASIAN DEVELOPMENT BANK

CONTENTS

TABLE AND FIGURES

ABBREVIATIONS

ADB	–	Asian Development Bank
APYS	–	Asia Pacific Youth Symposium
CBO	–	community-based organization
CDC	–	community development council
COVID-19	–	coronavirus disease
CPS	–	country partnership strategy
CSO	–	civil society organization
CWRD	–	Central and West Asia Department
DMC	–	developing member country
FCAS	–	fragile and conflict-affected situations
FPA	–	farmer professional association
IED	–	Independent Evaluation Department
M&E	–	monitoring and evaluation
NGO	–	nongovernment organization
NGOC	–	NGO and Civil Society Center
NIS	–	national integrity strategy
PCR	–	project completion report
PDA	–	pilot and demonstration activity
PRC	–	People's Republic of China
SARD	–	South Asia Department
SDG	–	Sustainable Development Goal
SERD	–	Southeast Asia Department
SIDS	–	small island developing states
TA	–	technical assistance
UNCAC	–	United Nations Convention against Corruption
WMCA	–	water management cooperative association
WUA	–	water user association
WWF	–	World Wide Fund for Nature
YFA	–	Youth for Asia

I. INTRODUCTION

In 2020, the Asian Development Bank (ADB) continued to engage civil society organizations (CSOs) in delivering development results.[1] ADB's Strategy 2030 continued to guide its cooperation with civil society as an approach to responding effectively to the changing development needs of its developing member countries (DMCs). Strategy 2030 recognizes that to deliver stronger, better, and faster, ADB must strengthen collaboration with a range of stakeholders, including CSOs. ADB aims to focus particularly on operations that use grassroots participatory approaches to target the poor and vulnerable groups, mobilize women and young people, and monitor project activities and outputs.[2]

Strategy 2030's operational priority 6 (strengthening governance and institutional capacity) further specifies that ADB will explore operational partnerships with civil society through streamlined grant processes and encourage citizens to become more involved in the design, implementation, and monitoring of ADB-financed operations and knowledge work. It states that ADB will develop operational approaches to directly engage with citizens by leveraging technology, crowdsourcing ideas from the youth, and working with smaller CSOs who represent groups of citizens and umbrella CSOs who draw together the perspectives of grassroots organizations. The NGO and Civil Society Center (NGOC) will continue to build upon existing good practices by sharing knowledge on how to successfully engage civil society and citizens in projects.[3] Strategy 2030's operational priority 1 (addressing remaining poverty and reducing inequality) also includes enhancing civil society engagement to promote participation and social inclusion, and to reduce inequalities as one of the strategies for achieving progress in the three operational areas. The operational priority 1 also cites enhancing partnerships with stakeholders, including CSOs, to generate knowledge, share good practices, and improve policy dialogue.[4]

[1] ADB. 2012. Strengthening Participation for Development Results: An Asian Development Bank Guide for Participation. Manila.

[2] ADB. 2018. Strategy 2030: Achieving a Prosperous, Inclusive, Resilient, and Sustainable Asia and the Pacific. Manila.

[3] ADB. 2019. Strategy 2030 Operational Plan for Priority 6: Strengthening Governance and Institutional Capacity, 2019–2024. Manila.

[4] ADB. 2019. Strategy 2030 Operational Plan for Priority 1: Addressing Remaining Poverty and Reducing Inequalities, 2019-2024. Manila.

Meaningful civil society engagement entails supporting ADB's DMCs in designing projects and developing policies that are participatory and socially inclusive (e.g., all genders, young and old, persons with disabilities, indigenous people, and the marginalized and most vulnerable). ADB asserts that the participation of CSOs contributes to effective, timely, and honest delivery of public services, accountability, transparency, and inclusivity. It also helps determine whether well-intentioned policies lead to desired development outcomes and meet citizen expectations (footnote 3). Furthermore, considering that CSOs play a vital role in organizing the community, efficiently connecting people with the market, and carrying out capacity development initiatives that can help the local community develop various social, capital, and human resources, CSOs can help DMCs achieve financial inclusion, particularly through microfinance.[5]

The coronavirus disease (COVID-19) pandemic radically transformed the way individuals, organizations, and communities operate. Adapting quickly has been difficult for countries in Asia and the Pacific. Many CSOs have demonstrated their abilities to respond to the changing needs of the poorest and most vulnerable, while maintaining the rigor of their development approach. The local knowledge and adaptability of CSOs demonstrate civil society's valuable role in responding to the ongoing pandemic. ADB must cooperate with CSOs for a range of reasons, including to tap their local knowledge, to build on their expertise, and to gain different perspectives in helping to address challenges under the current context.[6]

To account for ADB's increased commitment to CSO engagement, ADB approved in 2020 a new indicator for measuring civil society engagement in its portfolio. Previously, ADB measured civil society engagement by counting projects with planned CSO engagement of any type, typically registering over 90% of projects approved each year with planned activities for CSO participation. Starting in 2020, ADB is measuring what planned meaningful civil society engagement was delivered. Instead of reviewing documents that proposed activities, ADB now reviews the project completion reports (PCRs) of projects that close in a given year. ADB also defined that a project has meaningful CSO engagement if it rates "High" on Information Gathering and Sharing and on Consultation, and any level of Collaboration or Partnership approaches.[7] Of the 86 projects for which a PCR was prepared in 2020, 42 (49%) projects have planned meaningful civil society engagement in its original design. Of these 42 projects, 33 (79%) delivered their plans to involve CSOs through various engagement approaches. ADB believes that these figures more accurately represent the scope of CSO engagement in its portfolio.

---

5   C. Neriamparampil. 2020. How Civil Society Organizations Can Promote Financial Inclusion. *Development Asia: An Initiative of Asian Development Bank.* 27 March.

6   E. Thomas and L. Whitehead. 2020. Using the Flexibility of Civil Society to Overcome COVID-19. *Asian Development Blog.* 23 July.

7   ADB (NGOC). 2020. Request for Change in the Indicator of Civil Society Organization Engagement. Memorandum. 31 January (internal).

This year's report features case stories from these projects of how ADB involved CSOs throughout the project cycle by tapping their local knowledge, innovation, and expertise. For example, in Afghanistan, community development councils (CDCs) or *shuras* implemented subprojects on rehabilitation post-flooding. Water user associations (WUAs), many of which were led by women, received training on water resources management and how to operate subproject irrigation facilities in the Qinghai Province of the People's Republic of China (PRC). Two projects in Bangladesh reported high levels of CSO participation, one of which included organizing water management cooperative associations (WMCAs) to operate small-scale water resource infrastructure. The other project features a government–CSO partnership in monitoring corruption cases under the country's Good Governance Program. In the Philippines, the ADB project team extensively consulted and involved CSOs and people's organizations for rehabilitation interventions post-Typhoon Yolanda at local and national levels by tapping on the existing Kapit-Bisig Laban sa Kahirapan (Linking Arms Against Poverty)–Comprehensive and Integrated Delivery of Social Services program of the social welfare and development department. CSOs implemented resettlement plan in Viet Nam's Greater Mekong Subregion Expressway Project. A CSO focused on the welfare of persons with disabilities provided inputs to the construction design of sanitation facilities, while another CSO conducted water, sanitation, and hygiene training for communities under the Port Vila urban development project in Vanuatu.

Further in this report, civil society representatives participated in crafting country partnership strategies (CPSs) in Mongolia and Viet Nam. CSOs actively contributed their perspectives through stakeholders' consultations in three ongoing key policy and program reviews: Energy Policy review, Safeguard Policy Statement review, and Fragile and Conflict-Affected States Approach review. Resource persons from CSOs supported training and knowledge events for ADB staff on civil society engagement, Global Road Safety Partnership (GRSP), and the International Day Against Homophobia, Transphobia and Biphobia (IDAHOTB). Key CSO partners, World Wide Func for Nature (WWF) and Plan International, also reported on their key contributions to this year's ADB initiatives on sustainable management of natural resources (WWF) and youth engagement (Plan International).

The NGOC spearheads ADB's engagement with civil society, facilitating the involvement of CSOs in the design, implementation, and monitoring of ADB-financed projects. It works with the ADB-wide CSO Cooperation Network, composed of ADB specialists and officers from the headquarters and resident missions who are the focal persons for CSO engagement. The NGOC also leads ADB's engagement with youth groups in its portfolio in many ways through the Youth for Asia (YFA) initiative. This year, the YFA worked with various youth groups in facilitating intergenerational dialogues with ADB, DMCs, and CSOs for youth employment and livelihood in digital, informal, and green economies.

The NGOC has also pioneered an organization-wide mechanism for reviewing and advising on CSO engagement or the participation and empowerment components in ADB project documents, reports, and policy papers. In 2020, the NGOC reviewed and advised on CSO engagement components in 442 project documents. The review by the NGOC forwards a clearer description of CSO engagement and establishes a better baseline for future practice.

This report provides insights on ADB's cooperation with CSOs in 2020 and features lessons and success stories throughout Asia and the Pacific. It highlights important civil society contributions that have enabled ADB-financed operations to deliver better development outcomes.

II. SPOTLIGHT ON CIVIL SOCIETY ENGAGEMENT DURING THE PANDEMIC

Over the past decade, many local CSOs have been the first responders following a disaster or an emergency event in the region. Similarly, CSOs have taken action when the COVID-19 pandemic broke out in 2020, particularly focusing on areas that could not be reached by government services. Recognizing the role and efforts of many CSOs on the COVID-19 response, ADB approved in 2020 the technical assistance (TA) project on Mitigating the Impact of COVID-19 through Community-Led Interventions.[8] It directly supports CSOs in upscaling or expanding their ongoing health-focused interventions to respond to the pandemic between 2021 and 2023. It will deliver the following outputs: (i) community-based crisis prevention, mitigation, and adaptation increased; (ii) informal social protection programs stressed by COVID-19 supported; and (iii) economic support provided for people whose livelihoods are affected by COVID-19. More than 500 individuals from CSOs in 12 target countries registered for the online information session held in December 2020 about this project, with 85% stating they were delivering an ongoing COVID-19 response and wanted support to upscale their interventions. More than 300 individuals and organizations from various countries joined the webinar. Over 100 organizations submitted their project concepts. This high interest from the CSO sector demonstrates the considerable action from local and national CSOs to ease the impact of the pandemic on the most vulnerable communities. Efforts are ongoing, and CSOs need further support to replicate and scale up their initiatives.

An example of how CSOs are involved in ADB's COVID-19 response is the COVID-19 Active Response and Expenditure Support (CARES) Program in Cambodia. The program, a $250 million loan, will strengthen the country's health-care system, provide social assistance to the poor and vulnerable, and provide economic stimulus to businesses, including support to small and medium-sized enterprises. A country engagement framework guides the implementation of the program, which involves three subcommittees to provide oversight, including a civil society subcommittee.[9] Chaired by the ADB Cambodia country director and the secretary of state from the Ministry of Economy and Finance, the committee seeks inputs from CSOs to better understand the implementation challenges and successes in the rollout of

---

[8] ADB. 2020. Technical Assistance for Mitigating the Impact of COVID-19 through Community-Led Interventions. Manila.

[9] Multistakeholder Country Engagement Frameworks have been established in five countries in Southeast Asia: Cambodia, Indonesia, Myanmar, the Philippines, and Thailand.

COVID 19—Cambodia. ACLEDA Bank staff taking temperature checks before entering the office premise on 22 July 2020, Phnom Penh, Cambodia (photo by ADB).

post-COVID-19 response measures under the project. The committee's key tasks are to (i) facilitate partnership and interaction with the CSO community; (ii) formulate fast, transparent, efficient, and effective ways to serve and better understand communities in critical COVID-19-related activities; and (iii) provide a platform for further dialogue and engagement to better understand the impacts on adversely affected people. The CSO subcommittee has been instrumental in highlighting the need for more innovative and inclusive approaches to reach the poorest, and the need for improved access to information on existing government support measures and transparency to help address existing gaps. The subcommittee met for the first time in November 2020, which comprised both local and international nongovernment organizations (NGOs) and reflected the diverse stakeholder group. The subcommittee is expected to meet quarterly.[10]

Another example of civil society engagement in the COVID-19 response is the multimedia communications campaign that ADB supported in Mongolia to improve the reporting of domestic violence cases during the COVID-19 crisis. The campaign reaches out to women and children, advising them when to report, where to call, and where to ask for help. Both the CSO National Center Against Violence and the government agency, National Legal Institute, host digital platforms and websites where those at risk of violence can download information or report cases. The campaign beefed up the existing national phone-based reporting system by setting up chatbots, mobile applications, private chat groups, websites, and social media pages, while still keeping privacy protocols to protect the identities of those

---

[10] ADB. Cambodia: COVID-19 Active Response and Expenditure Support Program.

reporting. This $400,000 TA project supports the government's central database that captures all calls, whether from the domestic violence hotline 107, police hotline 102, legal call center, CSO hotline websites, and chatbots. ADB also supports domestic violence response operations and procures personal protective equipment and first-aid kits for shelters for the survivors. The initiative further supports frontline service providers through virtual training on mental health and stress management.[11]

Furthermore, ADB is a frontrunner in vaccine financing and possible distribution in the region, where engaging CSOs for information campaigns on the distribution strategy and addressing vaccine hesitancy may be vital in enhancing vaccine access.[12] CSOs may also be tapped for their important role of monitoring the transparency and accountability of ADB-supported COVID-19 projects and even the use of COVID-19 budgets of governments. At this time when ADB finds it challenging to send its teams for monitoring missions, it can engage and train partners from local CSOs and academe on project monitoring and evaluation (M&E), so they can support field monitoring while the bank does its M&E processes remotely. The TA that ADB provides DMCs on the use of information and communication technology, digital tagging of projects, and satellite technology for M&E may involve CSOs on the ground to complement these monitoring initiatives.

[11]   ADB. 2020. Preventing Domestic Violence amid COVID-19 in Mongolia. News article. 25 November.
[12]   ADB. 2020. ADB's Support to Enhance COVID-19 Vaccine Access. Manila.

III. ADB'S APPROACH TO CAPTURING CIVIL SOCIETY ENGAGEMENT

Since 2001, when ADB first reported on the extent of CSO participation in its portfolio, it has reported annually the planned CSO engagement, but did not track the delivery of that intent to invite CSOs to participate in project processes. Using a new indicator in 2020, ADB now tracks the percentage of completed projects that delivered meaningful CSO engagement out of the total number of completed projects which had planned to do so. ADB defines meaningful CSO engagement as significant information sharing or consultation activities, or any type of collaboration or partnership with CSOs, as seen in the table on p. 9.[13]

Forty-two of the 86 projects (49%) for which PCRs were prepared in 2020 described planned and meaningful civil society engagement in their project documents. Of these 42 projects, 33 or 79% delivered on these plans. These numbers are lower than those from the analysis using the old indicator. The decline in the figures based on the new indicator of meaningful CSO participation does not necessarily indicate a de facto decrease in the number and quality of civil society engagement in the ADB project portfolio. Instead, the new indicator gives more comprehensive information on the dimensions of CSO engagement, which has not been previously scrutinized. This change in the resulting figures on CSO engagement reflects ADB's shift in focus on quality over volume in evaluating its development results. By applying the new indicator and reviewing the quality of CSO engagements as delivered, project teams will be able to learn from past insights and plan for more relevant CSO activities in the future.

Figure 1 shows that the South Asia Department (SARD) had the highest number of projects with planned CSO engagement, as documented in 21 of 36 (58%) project planning documents. Of the 21 projects in SARD with planned CSO engagement, 19 (90%) delivered the planned CSO engagement. SARD is followed by the Central and West Asia Department (CWRD), where 10 of the 15 projects (67%) that closed in 2020 had planned CSO engagement. Of the 10 projects, 6 (60%) delivered their planned activities with CSOs. Following this is the Southeast Asia Department (SERD), with 7 of 15 projects (47%) having planned CSO engagement and 71% (5 of 7 projects) having implemented their plans. The East Asia Department (EARD) delivered 100% on its planned civil society engagement, although only 2 of the 15 projects that published their PCRs in the region planned to deliver meaningful CSO engagement.

---

[13] ADB (NGOC). 2020. Request for Change in the Indicator of Civil Society Organization Engagement. Memorandum. 31 January (internal).

Different Approaches and Depths of Participation

Approach	Definition[a]	Processing	Implementation
Information Generation and Sharing	Information is (i) generated by ADB, recipient, or client and shared with stakeholders; (ii) independently generated by stakeholders and shared with ADB, recipient, or client; or (iii) jointly produced.	**Low:** ADB, recipient, or client shares information with stakeholders **Medium:** Opportunity for stakeholders to share information with ADB, recipient, or client **High:** Joint generation and sharing of information to meet shared objectives (e.g., improved understanding)	**Low:** ADB, recipient, or client shares information with stakeholders **Medium:** Opportunities for civil society to share information with ADB, recipient, or client **High:** Joint generation and sharing of information to meet shared objectives (e.g., improved understanding)
Consultation	Stakeholder input is requested and considered as part of an inclusive policy, program, or project decision-making process.	**Low:** Web-based or written consultation only **Medium:** Opportunities for two-way face-to-face exchanges (e.g., workshop, focus group) **High:** Views of marginalized groups incorporated into design (e.g., use participatory methods)	**Low:** Web-based or written consultation only **Medium:** Opportunities for two-way face-to-face exchanges (e.g., workshop) **High:** Regular feedback from marginalized groups integrated during implementation (e.g., use participatory methods)
Collaboration	Stakeholders and ADB, recipient, or client work jointly, but stakeholders have limited control over decision-making and resources.	**Low:** Inputs from specific key stakeholders sought in project design **Medium:** Significant stakeholder representation on project design body **High:** Stakeholder influence on project design body and agreement of role for stakeholders in project implementation	**Low:** Stakeholder input in monitoring and evaluation **Medium:** Stakeholder organization (e.g., CSO) implementation of a project component **High:** Significant stakeholder representation on project implementation body and participation in implementation activities
Partnership	Stakeholders participate in decision-making process and/or exert control over resources, through a formal or informal agreement to work together toward common objectives.	**Low:** Agree a stakeholder organization will partner in ADB-funded project **Medium:** MOU or partnership agreed or stakeholders take some degree of direct responsibility **High:** MOU or partnership agreement negotiated including cofinancing and management, or stakeholders assume high level of ownership or responsibility	**Low:** Stakeholder organization routinely provides inputs and is recognized as a partner in ADB-funded project **Medium:** MOU or partnership agreement implemented, or stakeholders take some degree of direct responsibility **High:** MOU or partnership agreement implemented including financing and management, or stakeholders assume high level of ownership or responsibility

ADB = Asian Development Bank, CSO = civil society organization, MOU = memorandum of understanding.

[a] These generic definitions can be developed for particular types of projects (e.g., rural water supply), priority operational themes (e.g., gender), or individual projects.

Source: ADB. 2012. Strengthening Participation for Development Results: An Asian Development Bank Guide for Participation. Manila.

Figure 1: Projects with Planned Meaningful Civil Society Engagement in Project Completion Reports Delivered in 2020, by Regional Department

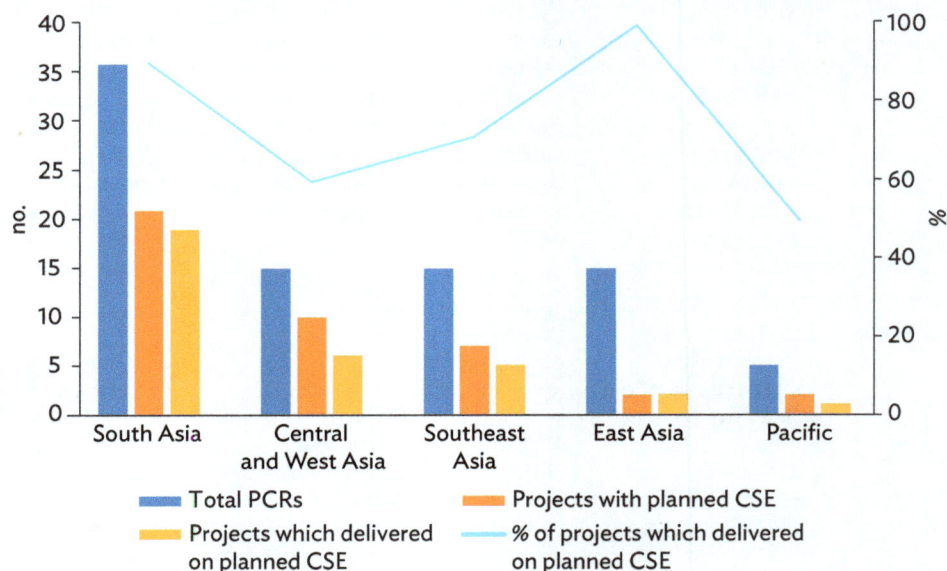

CSE = civil society engagement, PCR = project completion report.
Source: Asian Development Bank.

Figure 2 reflects that the two sectors with the highest number of projects with planned meaningful CSO engagement are agriculture and natural resources (9 projects or 21% of all projects with planned CSO engagement), and transport (9 or 21%). These are followed by education (6 or 14%) and water (5 or 12%). Projects in these sectors comprise 69% of those with planned meaningful CSO engagement. Of these, 100% of the projects in the water and education sectors delivered on their planned CSO engagement, while 89% of projects in agriculture and natural resources, and 67% of projects in the transport sector delivered on their plans. ADB project teams were able to incorporate more and capable project stakeholders from education and water due to the great number of nonprofit CSOs in these sectors.

In Figure 3, loans are the type of modality having the highest number of projects with planned meaningful CSO engagement (16 projects or 38%). Among four types of modality, projects financed through loans also have the highest delivery rate of planned meaningful CSO engagement (88%, 14 projects out of 16). The delivery rates are also high in projects financed through grants (83%, 5 projects out of 6) and a combination of grants and loans (75%, 6 projects out of 8). Projects financed through multitranche financing facility have the lowest delivery rate of planned meaningful CSO engagement (67%, 8 projects out of 12).

CSOs have taken diverse roles and responsibilities in ADB's project portfolio based on PCRs published in 2020, as reflected in Figure 4. CSOs have played the following four major roles in the 33 projects that delivered their planned meaningful CSO

**Figure 2: Civil Society Engagement in Projects
as Planned versus as Delivered in 2020, by Sector**

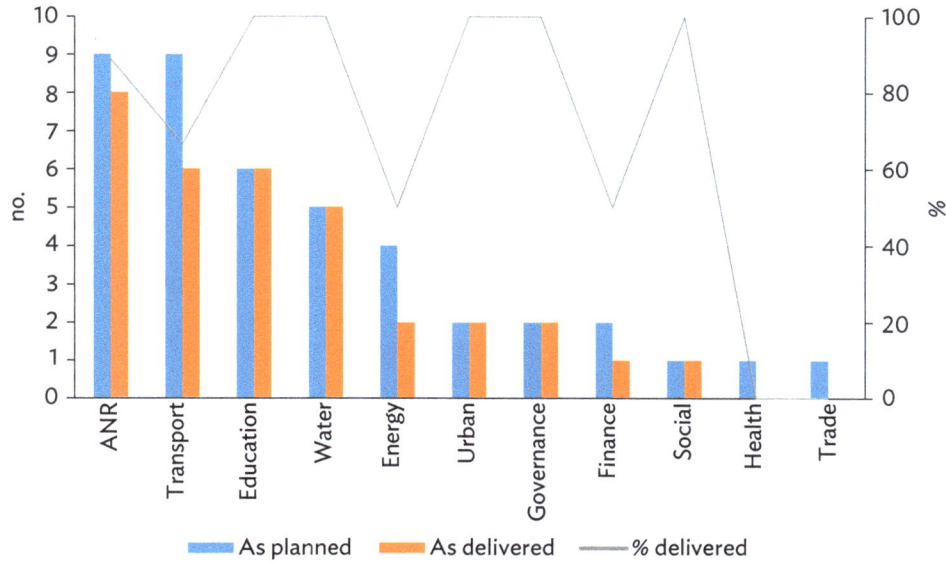

ANR = agriculture and natural resources.
Source: Asian Development Bank.

**Figure 3: Projects with Planned Meaningful Civil Society
Engagement in Project Completion Reports in 2020, by Modality**

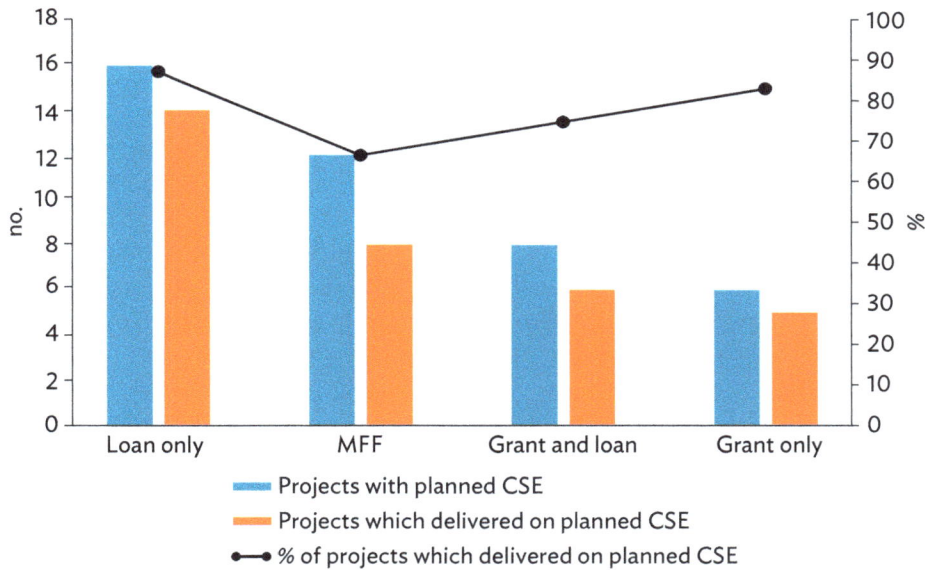

CSE = civil society engagement, MFF = multitranche financing facility.
Source: Asian Development Bank.

Figure 4: Roles of Civil Society Organizations in Projects That Delivered Meaningful Engagement Based on Project Completion Reports, 2020

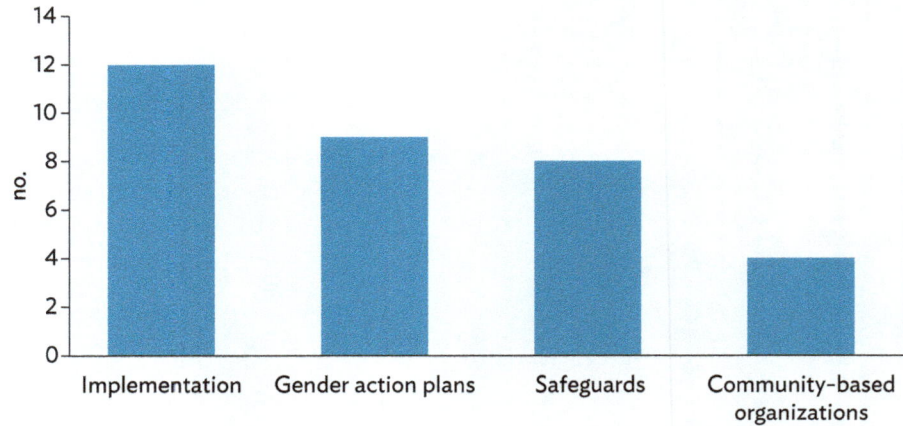

Source: Asian Development Bank.

engagement: (i) implementing some components of the projects (12 projects or 36%); (ii) designing or implementing gender action plans (9 projects or 27%); (iii) socioeconomic impact analysis at project design phase and designing and/or implementing the projects' environmental and social safeguards framework or plan, including the resettlement plans (8 projects or 24%); and (iv) capacity development and formation of grassroots or community-based organizations (CBOs) (4 projects or 12%). The projects, which involved CSOs for implementation of specific project components, are mainly from these sectors: agriculture and natural resources (4), education (4), water (2), urban (1), and finance (1).

The nine projects for which CSOs played a role in designing or implementing gender action plans are from these sectors: transportation (3), education (2), water (2), energy (1), and governance (1). CSOs were involved in designing or implementing gender action plans by participating in consultations, supporting public awareness campaigns, providing training, and conducting M&E activities. CBOs have played an active role as well. In the Water Supply and Sanitation Services Investment Program Project of Uzbekistan, for example, over 70 water consumer groups (WCGs), of which 57% of members are women, were formed in project areas to conduct awareness campaigns about gender, sanitation, and hygiene.

Projects from these sectors—transportation (3), agriculture and natural resources (1), water (1), energy (1), governance (1) and urban (1)—had CSOs involved in supporting the design and implementation of environmental and social safeguards. It is noteworthy that some projects directly contributed to the formation of grassroots or CBOs, mostly in the agriculture and natural resources and social sectors. This reflects direct involvement of local communities and farmer groups, who are important actors from these two sectors, in ADB-financed projects.

In terms of the tasks performed by CSOs, most (10 projects or 30%) delivered services, as reflected in Figure 5. Others performed tasks on monitoring (6 projects or 18%), resettlement (4 projects or 12%), training (4 projects or 12%), awareness-raising (4 projects or 12%), community organizing of grassroots or CBOs (4 projects or 12%), and needs assessment (1 project or 3%).

Figure 5: Tasks Performed by Civil Society Organizations in Projects That Delivered Meaningful Civil Society Engagement

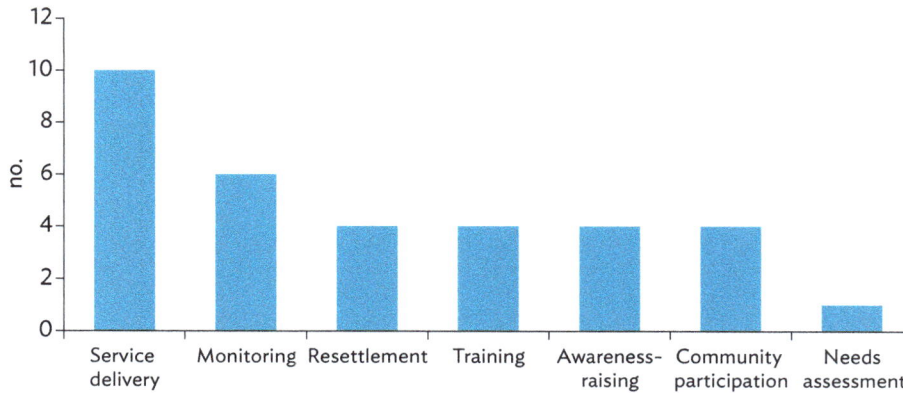

Source: Asian Development Bank.

CSOs participate in ADB projects through four approaches, as listed in the table on p. 9 and as presented in Figure 6, and have generally engaged through one or a combination of these approaches. Fifty percent of completed projects (42 projects) in 2020 planned for significant levels of the first three approaches: information generation and sharing, consultation, and collaboration. Half of these (or 21 projects) delivered on these plans, while the other half facilitated some levels of consultations with CSOs as the most frequently adopted approach. Only four projects planned to engage CSOs through partnership; nonetheless, all four projects delivered on this plan. Of the four approaches, building partnership represents the highest form of CSO engagement, which is more complex and requires greater effort to accomplish. Thus, there were fewer projects employing this approach. Nevertheless, the four projects, which originally planned for partnerships with CSOs at project design stage, appear to demonstrate appreciation of the contributions of CSOs in the delivery of project results and were committed to pursue these engagements until project completion. These four projects are (i) the Northern Flood-Damaged Infrastructure Emergency Rehabilitation Project in Afghanistan, (ii) the Skills Development Project in Nepal, (iii) the Education Sector Development Program in Sri Lanka, and (iv) the Kapit-Bisig Laban sa Kahirapan (Linking Arms Against Poverty)–Comprehensive and Integrated Delivery of Social Services National Community-Driven Development Program in the Philippines.

Figure 6: Types of Civil Society Organizations' Participation Approaches Adopted by 42 Projects with Planned Meaningful Civil Society Engagement in 2020

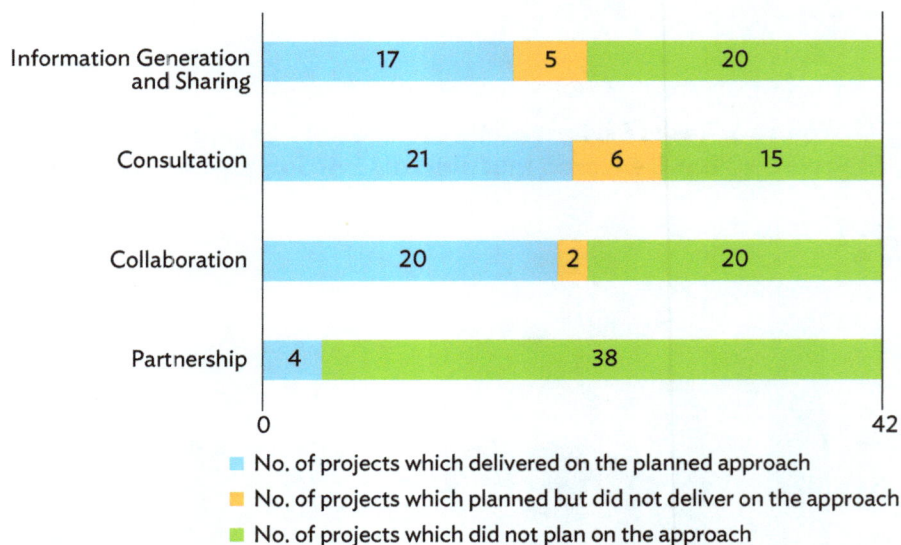

Source: Asian Development Bank.

Looking more closely at selected projects, there were various reasons why some projects were not able to deliver on their planned CSO engagement. These can be summarized as lack of readiness or limited preparation from either the project team or the CSO side of the engagement. For example, in one project, activities were implemented, not by CSOs as originally planned but by social safeguards officers and a private firm. Two projects cited limited capacity of local NGOs to support project activities; one of which originally planned to work with a more stable international NGO but decided to work with local groups. The project on health cited that, even though there were qualified local CSOs to work with, the project team encountered legal restrictions in contracting local CSOs, or some of the CSOs were not ready with the complexities involved in contracting with ADB. One project reallocated consultancy services to procuring three individual consultants instead of 10 NGOs for better management and coordination of project activities. Another project cited challenges in coordinating with large public transport sector workers groups.

IV. STORIES OF CHANGE— CIVIL SOCIETY ENGAGEMENT IN PRACTICE

The following select case stories illustrate meaningful civil society engagement, reflecting various approaches to CSO participation in ADB-financed projects and the range of ways that CSOs contribute to ADB's development targets. These case stories are collected from projects, which published their completion reports in 2020 in ADB's five regional departments.

A. Central and West Asia

Afghanistan: Working with *shuras* on infrastructure emergency rehabilitation. The Northern Flood-Damaged Infrastructure Emergency Rehabilitation Project in Afghanistan supported government efforts in the rehabilitation of irrigation and road infrastructure damaged by the severe flooding in northern Afghanistan between March and June 2014.[14] The project helped rehabilitate small-scale irrigation system and rural road infrastructure in 15 of the worst-affected provinces and larger-scale irrigation system infrastructure in three provinces. The overall project is rated *successful*, assessed as designed well and implemented as planned. The project had a significant impact on the target beneficiaries, and it fully achieved or even exceeded targets in several project indicators.

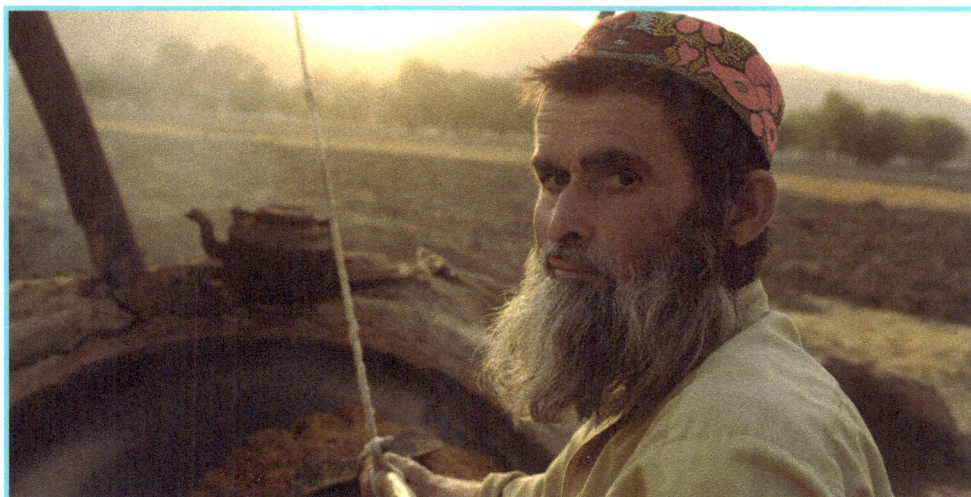

Northern flood-damaged infrastructure emergency rehabilitation project in Afghanistan. Afghan farmer prepares grain to sell at the flood protected land in Takhar. (photo by Jawad Jawali).

---

[14] ADB. 2020. Completion Report: Northern Flood-Damaged Infrastructure Emergency Rehabilitation Project in Afghanistan. Manila.

Because of the comprehensive community-level interventions required for the rehabilitation project, traditional community development councils (CDCs) or *shuras* extensively participated in project design consultations and delivered community-level small infrastructures. The Ministry of Rural Rehabilitation and Development contracted 853 CDCs on subproject interventions, which created at least 81,000 short-term and permanent jobs in the community. The contracting scheme with CDCs for subprojects generated direct and indirect employment during construction, and built CDC capacity and project ownership, with CDCs contributing up to 10% of the project costs. This arrangement with CDCs can be used in other community and project interventions post-project. Community leaders participated in the decision-making process on the subprojects, particularly during subproject selection and preparatory phases, and implementation. Women leaders also participated in the decision-making and implementation of subprojects (footnote 14).

B.   East Asia

People's Republic of China: Organizing rural water user associations for water resources management. Qinghai is among the poorest provinces in the PRC because of its remote location, mountainous landscape, and extreme climate. Agriculture is the main economic activity, but productivity is low because of poor water supply and agronomic practices. The Qinghai Rural Water Resources Management project contributed to increasing agricultural productivity and increasing farmers' income in Hualong, Jianzha, and Xunhua in Qinghai Province by establishing climate-resilient irrigation infrastructure, setting up participatory irrigation management, and providing agricultural services support for farmers.

Water resources management project in Qinghai Province. The Qinghai Rural Water Resources Management project contributed to increasing both agricultural productivity and farmers' income (photo by ADB East Asia Department).

As part of the participatory irrigation management activities, the project supported the establishment and registration of 12 model water users associations (WUAs), providing them office space and supporting them in setting up their charters and operating procedures. The WUAs' members reached a total of 19,120, among whom ethnic minorities accounted for 97%.[15] WUA farmers participated in training programs to operate and manage irrigation plans and water delivery schedules. Four model WUAs signed service contracts with a service delivery organization. They received further advanced training on the operation of main irrigation canals, as well as on irrigation management and techniques. Field trials introduced and demonstrated water conservation measures, and county governments provided water-saving rewards to encourage wider uptake of these practices. With the improved irrigation system, the project reduced the persistent water scarcity and disputes over water sharing and distribution.

Increasing access to water fostered social cohesion and contributed to forming self-sustaining and self-reliant farmers' groups and developing the capacity of farmer professional associations (FPAs). In collaboration with WUAs and FPAs, the project provided field demonstrations to successful farm areas and trainings on integrated pest management, on-farm water management, and cropping calendar management. These training programs have improved the technical and managerial capacities of FPAs and WUAs, which helped facilitate farmers' access to agricultural

Participatory rapid assessment meeting with farmers. The project supported the establishment and registration of model water user associations whose members are mostly ethnic minorities (photo by ADB East Asia Department).

---

15 ADB. 2020. Completion Report: Qinghai Rural Water Resources Management Project in the People's Republic of China. Manila.

inputs and other services. It also helped farmers negotiate better deals with providers and enhance their accountability to their clients.

As women take leading roles in agricultural production and irrigation, the project ensured women's membership in WUAs and FPAs and their participation in decision-making. The 12 WUAs established have 9,250 female members, representing 48% of the total membership. Women represented 30% of the leading members of model WUAs; 1,731 women (48%) participated in the project's irrigation management training, while 4,698 (36%) women joined the FPAs village projects and training activities, particularly on improving their agriculture marketing skills (footnote 15).

C.   South Asia

Bangladesh: Participatory approach to managing small-scale water facilities.
The Participatory Small-Scale Water Resources Sector Project contributed to the Government of Bangladesh's and ADB's policies on poverty reduction through sustainable agricultural production. The project was well-designed, implemented efficiently, and on time. It developed a strong institutional setup of 412 water management cooperative associations (WMCAs). Thirty seven percent of WMCA members are women who are capable of operating and maintaining the infrastructures through robust operations and management plans. Among its innovations are providing microcredit schemes through the WMCAs and having the beneficiaries monitor the quality of construction of the small-scale water resource infrastructures under the project.

Bangladesh small-scale water facility. The project contributed to the government's and ADB's aim to address poverty by supporting agricultural production (photo by ADB South Asia Department).

Engaging CSOs as consultants as well as implementing partner organizations helped deliver the project results effectively. In particular, several CSOs, such as the Bangladesh Association for Social Advancement, Bangladesh Centre for Advancement Studies, Country Vision, and Voluntary Association for Family Welfare and Social Development, conducted participatory rural appraisal with rural stakeholders. The appraisals led to integrating the interest of the poor households in project design. The project also engaged the Christian Commission for Development in Bangladesh to implement the resettlement plan. Furthermore, consultants from the Employment and Technology Development Agency, Health and Education for the Local Underprivileged People (HELP), and Center for Environmental and Geographic Information Services (CEGIS) trained community assistants to build capacities of WMCAs on agriculture and fisheries extension program, operate and manage small-scale water resource facilities, and conduct the project impact evaluation.[16]

Bangladesh: Mobilizing civil society organizations and other stakeholders for good governance. The Good Governance Program in Bangladesh successfully supported the government's and ADB's strategy for governance reforms and countering endemic and widespread corruption. Continued policy dialogue, not only with the government but also with other stakeholders, such as the judiciary, civil society, and other development partners, will sustain the reforms that the program helped install.[17]

Engaging civil society organizations to deliver training. The Bangladesh small-scale water facility project trained men and women on agriculture and fisheries extension program (photo by ADB South Asia Department).

[16] ADB. 2020. Completion Report: Participatory Small-Scale Water Resources Sector Project in Bangladesh. Manila.
[17] ADB. 2020. Completion Report: Good Governance Program in Bangladesh. Manila.

The government has recognized the substantive role of civil society in fighting corruption. The Anticorruption Commission has put in place mechanisms to partner with CSOs and other stakeholders in fighting corruption at the local levels. Civil society and media are able to independently call on cases of corruption across the country, as reflected in the work of the Committee of Concerned Citizens and as supported by the Transparency International Bangladesh. The program's innovative features include establishing a national integrity strategy (NIS) that is aligned with the United Nations Convention against Corruption (UNCAC) and developing close coordination with NGOs and CSOs to critically assess corruption vulnerability. The NIS is owned by the National Integrity Advisory Council at the highest level of government. The UNCAC Civil Society Coalition Report 2011 confirmed that Bangladesh's legal regime largely complies with the standards and principles of the UNCAC. Three independent reviews, supported by CSOs, reported of extensive collaboration and coordination with development partners and civil society in the implementation of the NIS, performance of UNCAC and anticorruption work, and extent of community outreach and corruption prevention activities, including partnership modalities of anticorruption agencies with civil society.

The CSOs supported the preparation of citizen report cards on service delivery and helped organize public consultations on the NIS. To sustain support by future governments, the program instituted mechanisms for capacity development and extensive policy dialogues with stakeholders, including development partners and civil society, wide consultations with bureaucracy, and involvement of leaders of various government agencies (footnote 17).

D.   Southeast Asia

Philippines: Supporting community resilience to disasters. Between 2014 and 2018, ADB's emergency loan assistance supported 512 municipalities affected by the 2013 Typhoon Yolanda in the Philippines. The project used the established Kapit-Bisig Laban sa Kahirapan (Linking Arms Against Poverty)–Comprehensive and Integrated Delivery of Social Services program of the Department of Social Welfare and Development to deliver the project's interventions for recovery and rehabilitation. The project aimed to increase the access of affected households to basic services and infrastructure such as roads, education, health centers, and water through participatory community development approaches.[18]

The project involved extensive civil society and community participation at various levels. CSO representatives became members of various project structures, including the municipal and national steering committees. All (100%) of the covered municipalities saw increased membership of individual citizens and CSOs in the local development councils and special bodies as against a target of 85%. CSOs

---

[18]   ADB. 2020. Completion Report: KALAHI–CIDSS National Community-Driven Development Project in the Philippines. Manila.

participated in planning the framework for engaging community volunteers in all target barangays (villages), which organized committees to undertake specific tasks during project planning and implementation. Many of these committees have transformed into formal people's organizations to sustain the operation and maintenance of subprojects, such as parent–teacher associations, maintaining school buildings, and community enterprise groups for postharvest facilities.

The project also exceeded targets on women's participation. The project trained an average of 29 community volunteers per barangay on community organizing skills; 64% were women, as against a target of 10 volunteers per barangay with *50% women*. A total of 189,872 volunteers occupied leadership positions as chairpersons in the volunteer committees; about 113,209 or 60% are women, compared to a *50% target* (footnote 18).

Viet Nam: Increasing trade and competitiveness in the Greater Mekong Subregion. The Greater Mekong Subregion Ben Luc–Long Thanh Expressway Project aimed to promote sustainable economic growth and regional cooperation by expanding access to markets, facilitating the movement of goods and people, and helping improve connectivity in the Greater Mekong Subregion. The project anticipated a more efficient and safer movement of goods and people in the greater Ho Chi Minh City. The project consulted with CBOs and affected populations at various stages of the project implementation. As part of the Resettlement Plan, the project provided a capacity-building program on resettlement and livelihood for women and households headed by women in all covered districts, in close cooperation with women's unions. The committees of income restoration program included the representatives of women's unions in the project districts. Representatives of women's unions and farmers' associations also sit in the District Compensation and Site Clearance Committees during resettlement and income restoration program implementation.[19]

E.   Pacific

Vanuatu: Civil society organizations and urban development. The Port Vila Urban Development Project in Vanuatu addressed Port Vila's most urgent basic urban needs of roads, drainage, and community sanitation facilities. The project was relevant to the country's development priorities and ADB's country strategy, implemented efficiently within the budget and time frame, and substantially achieved the targeted development impact.[20] With the collaborative efforts of ADB and the cofinanciers—the Government of Australia and the Global Environment Facility—the project provided essential urban services and facilities, including upgrading roads to improve transportation, constructing and rehabilitating drainage

---

[19]   ADB. 2020. Completion Report: Greater Mekong Subregion Ben Luc-Long Thanh Expressway Project – Tranche 1 in Viet Nam. Manila.
[20]   ADB. 2020. Completion Report: Port Vila Urban Development Project in Vanuatu. Manila.

systems to reduce flooding risk, establishing the fecal sludge treatment plant to collect and treat all fecal sludge, and constructing new and upgrading existing community sanitation facilities to improve community sanitation services and health. It is clear that the project has led to positive economic, environmental, social, and poverty reduction impacts.

The community-based elements of the project, delivered by CSOs, resulted in positive impacts for women and girls. An independent evaluation confirmed the increased awareness level of water, sanitation, and hygiene information and an anecdotal decrease in the incidence of diarrhea. In addition, communities were visibly cleaner—an issue that women and girls had highlighted during consultations. Finally, in Mele Waisisi and five other informal communities in the greater Port Vila area, the project supported installation of sanitation facilities near homes, when previously they used bush toilets.

Furthermore, the project extensively consulted with key stakeholders and ensured that the voice of women, as well as men, informed every step of project development, from site selection for community and public sanitation facilities to the initial design and subsequent revision of designs of these sanitation facilities. The Vanuatu Society of People with Disabilities played a key role in the site inspections to ensure that facilities were fully accessible. Women and girls in the communities benefited greatly from World Vision Vanuatu's nutrition information program. Women are now breastfeeding their infants longer after learning from the sanitation committees about the importance of breastfeeding a baby for at least 6 months. The project also contracted a local CSO, Wan Smolbag, for HIV and gender awareness sessions, targeting George Kalsakau Drive Concourse personnel and community partners (footnote 20).

V. PROMOTING ADB–CIVIL SOCIETY–GOVERNMENT COLLABORATION

A. Consulting Civil Society Organizations in Ongoing ADB Policy and Program Reviews

Safeguard Policy Statement Review. ADB is undertaking a comprehensive review to update its 2009 Safeguard Policy Statement (SPS). Civil society is expected to play a meaningful role in this review. The SPS looks at the impacts of ADB-supported projects on environment, involuntary resettlement, and indigenous peoples. In the 10 years of implementation of the policy, ADB has improved the capacity of DMCs and private sector clients to manage social and environmental risks of their development projects. With the changing context in countries and regions, the SPS needs to be updated to remain relevant and robust in responding to evolving development needs. ADB is committed to ensuring meaningful consultations throughout the policy review process to build on and learn from experiences and feedback from stakeholders across many perspectives and backgrounds. Thus, in 2020, ADB began the stakeholder engagement process with a small number of consultations and with the conceptualization of the stakeholder engagement plan for the policy review. The consultation process will be conducted in three phases. In the first phase, ADB launched the review and began to prepare the stakeholder engagement plan. In 2021, the review will include a series of internal and external stakeholder consultations with member countries, development partners, governments, the private sector, CSOs, project-affected persons, indigenous peoples, and vulnerable groups.

Energy Policy Review. ADB's Energy Policy 2009 provided the framework for ADB's assistance to its DMCs in the energy sector. In 2020, ADB's Independent Evaluation Department (IED) published the results of its sector-wide evaluation of the bank's Energy Policy and Program, 2009–2019. Among the IED's key recommendations is for ADB to revisit its energy policy and formally withdraw from financing new coal-fired energy capacity for the region to conform to the global consensus on climate change. ADB has not invested in coal-fired power plants since 2013 and now needs to align its policy to this practice. The IED's review found that ADB's energy program significantly contributed to meeting the electricity requirements of its DMCs. ADB invested in power grid infrastructure and increased the share of renewable energy in the region through public and private sector financing. However, while ADB is a pioneering investor in renewable energy, more investments are needed on demand-side efficiency, last-mile electrification, and sector reforms.

ADB's energy sector group has been consulting with various stakeholders, including CSOs, on the results of this independent review, with the intent of shaping its new energy policy. Between June and December 2020, ADB organized two online consultations with the NGO Forum on ADB and its key members from across Asia and the Pacific who are involved in the environment, debt, and energy policy advocacy campaigns. The CSOs welco capacity-building program on resettlement and livelihood for women and households headed by women in all covered districts med the recommendation of ADB's IED to withdraw from financing coal-fired energy projects. At the same time, they raised related concerns on (i) outstanding debt for coal-related transmission and distribution projects, (ii) the need to protect labor interest and ensure green jobs in a just transition to renewable energy, (iii) pitfalls of geothermal energy, (iv) the need to decentralize energy access, and (v) the need to focus on zero-waste technology solutions.[21]

Fragile and Conflict-Affected Situations and Small Island Developing States Approach. ADB's Strategy 2030 puts increasing emphasis on the need for a differentiated approach in fragile and conflict-affected situations (FCAS) and small island developing states (SIDS). ADB is developing a new FCAS and SIDS Approach to operationalize this mandate. In 2020, ADB kicked off the preparation of the FCAS and SIDS Approach with consultations across a wide range of stakeholder groups, including CSOs that operate in FCAS and SIDS. The first round of consultations, held in October and November 2020, asked participants to help define the scope of the FCAS and SIDS Approach and to share relevant civil society expertise in this area. In 2021, ADB will share the draft approach and host another round of consultations with civil society to seek their feedback.

B. Engaging Civil Society Organizations in Country Partnership Strategies

The country partnership strategy (CPS) is ADB's primary platform for designing operations to deliver development results at the country level. ADB works with each DMC to map out a medium-term development strategy and a 3-year country operations business plan to implement it.

In August 2020, as part of the formulation of the new CPS for Viet Nam, ADB's Viet Nam Resident Mission organized consultation meetings with NGOs, among other stakeholders. CSOs contributed to (i) identifying gender issues and presenting recommendations to promote gender equality in agriculture and natural resources management, environmental management, and in urban and water sectors; (ii) providing inputs for the Inclusive and Sustainable Growth Assessment; and (iii) providing inputs for country gender assessment and gender recommendations for ADB operations in Viet Nam. In January 2021, the Viet Nam Resident Mission CPS team conducted further consultations with CSOs to seek their inputs to the draft document and invited key Viet Nam CSOs working in ADB's operation sectors.

---

[21] ADB. Energy Policy Review (accessed 17 March 2021).

Consulting CSOs on country partnership strategies. The Mongolia Resident Mission consulted with civil society organizations on the education sector analysis for the country partnership strategy (photo by ADB).

In Mongolia, the Mongolia Resident Mission also organized a series of consultations with CSOs from April 2020 to December 2020 in formulating the CPS. More than 340 CSOs were invited and representatives from 161 organizations participated in this series of events—the final review of CPS 2017–2020 in April; the education sector analysis in May; the analyses of the gender sector, agriculture and natural resources sector, and health sector in June; poverty and social protection sector analysis in July; urban development sector and public administration sector analyses in September; and private sector development analysis in December 2020.[22]

C.   Youth for Asia Initiative and Promoting Meaningful Youth Engagement

The Youth for Asia (YFA) team of the NGOC facilitated intergenerational dialogues between ADB officers and staff, DMC representatives, and young leaders on expanding opportunities for the youth in the informal, digital, and green economies through its signature event, the Asia Pacific Youth Symposium (APYS). The YFA involved young people in the project design across some 10 projects in 2020 by working with select ADB operations departments, sectors, and thematic groups. It also contributed to research and knowledge work on the impact of the pandemic on young people across the region. Examples of the YFA events, project operational support, and knowledge work are provided.

[22]   As presented by the CSO Anchor from the Mongolia Resident Mission during the online 2020 CSO Anchors Training for ADB staff in November 2020.

Asia Pacific Youth Symposium. In coordination with the ADB Institute and Plan International, the YFA team organized its signature event from 12 August 2020 to 23 September 2020. The APYS event gathered over 950 participants from 50 DMCs for a cross-generational dialogue on meaningful youth engagement and youth economic empowerment in the new normal. The event's discussions centered around youth employment and livelihood in the digital, informal, and green economies in response to the COVID-19 pandemic.

The key messages for ADB, governments, CSOs, and other development partners arising from the APYS event series are (i) the need for more upskilling programs, which would develop relevant soft and technical skills for young people to fully participate in their economies; (ii) for CSOs and other development partners to support the plan and facilitate greater connection between young people and other stakeholders, such as the government and the private sector; and (iii) that youth-led and youth-focused CSOs can provide platforms for knowledge sharing among different sectors, and to include young people in the discussion. The YFA delivered the APYS event series online and leveraged platforms including Zoom, Miro, and social media to ensure greater reach and inclusivity. The APYS was the first ADB event that included sign language translations throughout, including in breakout discussion rooms. The event leveraged key engagements with the International Labour Organization; Organisation for Economic Co-operation and Development; Office of the United Nations Secretary General's Envoy on Youth; Office of the President of the Republic of Indonesia; Restless Development; Cambridge University; and the Youth Co:Lab initiative by the Citi Foundation and the United Nations Development Programme, which provided the speakers and resource persons; with the Special Olympics Asia Pacific and the Philippine National Association of Sign Language Interpreters for inclusive participation or involving young people with disabilities to participate in the events. The APYS was an interactive, visually engaging, and tech-savvy event.

Kathmandu's Youth-Led Approaches to Sustainable Bagmati River Improvement (Pilot and Demonstration). Supporting the Sustainable Bagmati River Basin Management Program, the youth-led pilot and demonstration activity (PDA) virtually trained 1,703 World's Largest Lesson participants (ages 13–24) through a 90-minute interactive module.[23] Another 196 participants underwent a more intensive 6-week training (ages 18–29) about the Sustainable Development Goals (SDGs) and 3R (reuse, reduce, and recycle) principles using intersector and intergenerational approaches. There were 107 locally trained youth facilitators and 10 SDGs training youth facilitators who implemented the training from August to November 2020. As a part of the SDGs training, more than 30 young people joined a virtual dialogue with officials from the government of Nepal, NGOs, CBOs and/or activists, and local politicians to discover new pathways to make the river healthy and clean by

---

[23] These activities were supported by the following TA projects: ADB. Regional: Demonstrating Innovative Employment Solutions through Regional Knowledge-Sharing Partnerships with Youth Organizations (TA 9557-REG); and ADB. Regional: Knowledge and Innovation Support for ADB's Water Financing Program (TA 6498-REG).

Asia Pacific Youth Symposium. Participating youth leaders call on ADB, governments, civil society organizations, and other development partners on the need for upskilling programs to build the technical and soft skills of young people to fully participate in their economies (photo by Youth for Asia).

strengthening ongoing initiatives and developing new collaborative spaces. By the end of the program, 32 youth-led project proposals were presented, of which 19 proposals proceeded to project implementation. The PDA demonstrated strong evidence of the value of engaging with young people in the SDGs and their effectiveness in building inclusive, sustainable, and climate change-resilient behaviors in local youth communities. The PDA recommended to replicate and upscale such youth-led programs and to continue the meaningful engagement of youth in taking actions to contribute to Agenda 2030 and the achievement of the SDGs.

Youth for Asia Knowledge Work on COVID-19. The YFA prepared a report assessing the damaging impacts of the COVID-19 pandemic on youth employment in the Asia and Pacific region, and recommending critical policy responses.[24]

---

24 C. Morris and F. Weidenkaff. 2020. Tackling the COVID-19 Youth Employment Crisis in the Asia and Pacific region. Manila: ADB / Bangkok: International Labour Organization.

The report, a collaboration between ADB and the International Labour Organization, finds that the employment prospects of the region's 660 million young people are severely challenged. They will be hit harder than adults and risk bearing higher and longer-term economic and social costs. The report urges governments to involve young people in policy and social dialogues and to adopt urgent, large-scale, and targeted interventions. Responses should focus on labor market policies, such as youth-targeted wage subsidies and public employment programs, and measures to lessen disruptions to education and training (footnote 24).

The YFA initiative also worked with young people of the region and prepared a series of blogs documenting the effect of the pandemic on the lives of young people and how young people, with their resilience, tenacity, and energy, are helping others to mitigate the effects of the pandemic. The YFA team published a blog, "Six ways young people are helping Asia through the pandemic," summarizing stories from six young people from across the region.[25]

D.   ADB Staff Training on Civil Society Engagement

Training on Impact for Results: Deepening Engagement with Civil Society. The NGOC delivered two training sessions for CSO anchors who comprise ADB's CSO Cooperation Network. CSO anchors are ADB specialists, officers, and consultants from headquarters and resident missions who are appointed focal persons on civil society engagement. The first session of the training, Impact for Results: Deepening Engagement with Civil Society, was an ADB-wide learning event held on 17–19 November 2020 with over 80 attendees, including CSO anchors and other ADB staff. The second session on 8–10 December 2020 focused on 36 CSO anchors and project staff from Central and West Asia Department (CWRD). NGOC delivered the training events online, which expanded the training beyond its usual target audience.

CSO Anchors Training. Representatives from ADB senior management, Sustainable Development and Climate Change Department (SDCC) Director General Woochong Um, SARD Director General Kenichi Yokoyama, and SERD Director General Ramesh Subramaniam shared their insights on involving CSOs in ADB's work. SERD CSO anchor Pinsuda Alexander moderated the panel discussions. They highlighted the potential roles of CSOs as ADB's eyes and ears on the ground, noting that CSOs can reach remote areas, identify ADB's blind spots, provide neutral oversight, and can, therefore, be tapped for monitoring ADB-supported projects. CSOs have important inputs and perspectives to ADB's work at policy and project levels and, thus, should be given space and opportunity to provide feedback on its work. An emerging space for feedback and communication with

---

[25] C. Morris and J. Sanvictores. 2020. *Six Ways Young People Are Helping Asia through the Pandemic.* Asian Development Blog. 20 July.

ADB management panelists in the CSO Anchors Training. SDCC Director General (DG) Woochong Um, SARD DG Kenichi Yokoyama and SERD DG Ramesh Subramaniam saying ADB has a role in facilitating dialogues between developing member countries and civil society organizations (photo by ADB NGO and Civil Society Center).

CSOs is the digital space, and ADB should continue to ensure that this space is transparent, inclusive, and accountable. ADB staff should also shift their mindsets on civil society engagement from "need" to "want," or from compliance with ADB's business processes to promoting CSO participation because it contributes to ADB's development results.

Oxfam's Asia Regional Director Lilian Mercado, India's Self-Employed Women's Association Chief Executive Officer Reema Nanavaty, and village leader Kapila Rasnon shared feedback on the situation of advocacy and service provider CSOs in the current pandemic context, the challenges and opportunities of engaging with ADB, and their recommendations for deepening ADB's cooperation with CSOs. SARD CSO anchor Francesco Tornieri moderated the panel discussions. They highlighted the need to support people's vaccines and to make sure no one will profiteer from vaccine procurement and distribution. They also called on ADB to help address the digital divide and support the protection of civic space. They said that while the work of CSOs had been gravely affected by the pandemic, many were able to respond quickly to the needs of the most vulnerable communities they are already working with, according to the resources and capacities they have. Some had to shift their community organization and communications work through online platforms. However, CSOs need further support from development partners to continue their work on these.

They further recommended the following to ADB: (i) to view the current pandemic as an opportunity for positive and creative disruption or "a great reset" of existing social, economic, political, and environmental systems that perpetuate inequality; (ii) citing its Strategy 2030, for ADB to recognize its role in ushering this creative disruption for change by supporting DMCs toward social inclusion and addressing

Dialogues between CSOs and ADB staff. Oxfam in Asia regional director Lilian Mercado, Self-Employed Women's Association chief Reema Nanavaty, and village leader Kapila Rasnon highlighted contributions of CSOs in development projects, and that empowerment of women should be at the heart of these projects (photo by ADB NGO and Civil Society Center).

inequalities.[26] The pandemic is not only a health crisis but a multidimensional crisis, which requires a comprehensive resetting of the societies' priorities and action; and (iii) for ADB to create instruments that can support community-based and grassroots organizations, which are on the front lines of development work.

On the other hand, CSO anchors from ADB's five regional operations shared their own experiences on engaging with CSOs. Their experiences in 2020 cited the following factors, which facilitated their engagement with CSOs:

(i)   localizing staff training on civil society engagement at resident missions, including translating learning materials into local languages;

(ii)   developing a database of CSO partners and supporting the creation of CSO advisory groups;

(iii)   providing training on safeguard monitoring for CSOs;

(iv)   contracting CSOs in project implementation and delivery;

(v)   involving CSOs in COVID-19 response in project implementation or oversight committees;

(vi)   consulting CSOs in FCAS program review and strategy formulation;

(vii)   providing training for governments on civil society engagement;

(viii)   reaching out to CSO umbrella organizations by participating in their activities and assemblies;

(ix)   supporting DMCs to set up CSO desks; and

(x)   making procurement guidelines more flexible to encourage CSO participation.

---

[26]   ADB. 2018. Strategy 2030: Achieving a Prosperous, Inclusive, Resilient, and Sustainable Asia and the Pacific. Manila. p. vi.

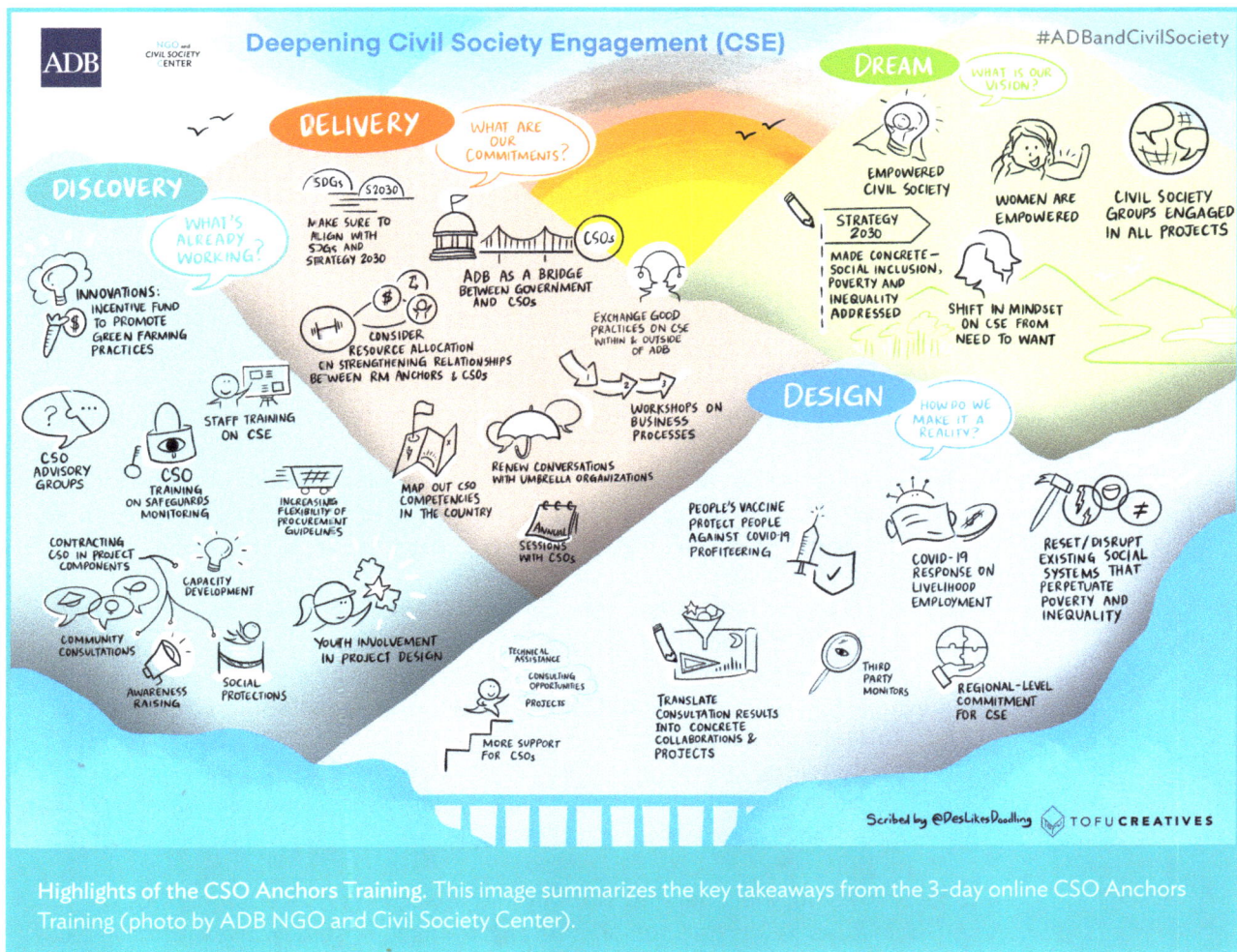

Highlights of the CSO Anchors Training. This image summarizes the key takeaways from the 3-day online CSO Anchors Training (photo by ADB NGO and Civil Society Center).

Central and West Asia Department Training. In the CWRD training on promoting CSO participation in ADB portfolio, CSO anchors from Afghanistan, Armenia, Tajikistan, and Uzbekistan, with the support of CWRD CSO anchor Aida Satylganova, presented case stories of their engagement with CSOs even under challenging contexts of conflict and the pandemic in the region. In Afghanistan, the ADB project team contracted more than 800 *shuras* to implement subprojects for the flooding rehabilitation project. The Armenia Resident Mission worked with the CSO Child Development Fund to support the education ministry's program on facilitating online learning under the pandemic context and providing psychosocial support for learners, teachers, and parents. In Tajikistan, two CSOs, the Fund for Poverty Reduction and the Analytical Center Navo, supported the tourism ministry in preparing the country's tourism profile and developing a sustainable tourism development plan. In Uzbekistan, the Khorezm Rural Advisory Support Services coordinated with various offices of the agriculture ministry to train farmers on livestock value chain development.

CSO leaders, Giorgi Kldiashvili of the Institute for the Development of Freedom of Information in Georgia and Lusine Simonyan of the Child Development Fund in Armenia, also discussed the situations of CSOs in the contexts of the pandemic and conflicts in the Central and West Asia region, and provided recommendations on how ADB can support their work. The following are some of their key suggestions for ADB:

(i)   elaborate on country-specific strategies for 2030 with the engagement of CSOs;
(ii) support institutional and capacity development of CSOs by providing opportunities for engagement in M&E of ongoing projects in the country;
(iii) support the creation of local and regional networks of CSOs, which concentrate on responsible business development and environmental protection;
(iv) listen to and understand the contexts and experiences of CSOs and integrate them into projects, and use ADB's network of experts to support CSOs in engaging with governments under the context of conflict during pandemic; and
(v)   support and further promote CSO involvement in government processes, such as in developing strategies and mechanisms to respond to crises created by conflicts and pandemic. ADB can discuss with government and negotiate involvement of CSOs in government development response strategies. ADB can tap CSO expertise in its projects with DMCs to have a consolidated approach in working with government. ADB can support CSO initiatives in working with their DMCs, such as the Open Parliament project, to promote government–CSO dialogue.

Global Road Safety Partnership Training. In November and December 2020, the Global Road Safety Partnership (GRSP) Training, hosted by the International Federation of Red Cross and Red Crescent Societies, conducted a sector and skills development program on behalf of the ADB Transport Sector Group. The program focused on road safety management and targeted participants holding leadership positions in road safety from DMCs and ADB staff who work on road safety-related projects. A key focus is outlining evidence-based interventions to achieve the targets set out in Sustainable Development Goal 3.6, which calls for a 50% reduction in road crash deaths by 2030. The program drew insights from experts within the GRSP, as well as another CSO, the Global New Car Assessment Program, and representatives from Johns Hopkins University and the Transport Accident Commission of Victoria, Australia.

E.   Knowledge Partnerships and Learning Events

Joint Activities with the WWF for Nature Building on 20 Years of Collaboration. In 2021, ADB and the WWF will mark 20 years of collaboration. The partnership is unique in its longevity and benefits from the depth of relationship built over this period. With the shared objective of promoting a green recovery from the COVID-19 pandemic, ADB and the WWF have a joint focus on sustainable infrastructure, nature-based solutions, the blue economy, and water resources management.

Water resources management. The WWF's Water Stewardship team worked with ADB's Water Sector Group and others to develop a draft Water Stewardship Program for ADB. This was structured around two key impact pathways: mobilizing financial flows for water stewardship, and scaling private sector investments via urban–basin links. The WWF anticipates working with ADB on rollout, focusing on implementation in India, Indonesia, Pakistan, the PRC, and Viet Nam. An example of implementation already underway is the TA project in Pakistan, Revitalizing the Ecosystem of Ravi River Basin, where the WWF-Pakistan provided research, advisory support, and stakeholder engagement to address industrial pollution. The outputs contributed to the industrial pollution hotspot maps and helped inform the planning process for the eco-revitalization plan. Discussions continue between the organizations and the Government of Pakistan about potential cooperation under the ReCharge Pakistan wet ands restoration project.

Healthy oceans and blue economy. The areas of cooperation under healthy oceans and blue economy have been focused on plastic pollution, coastal resilience, and blue finance. On reducing plastic pollution, the partnership is focusing on Indonesia, the PRC, the Philippines, Thailand, and Viet Nam. ADB and the WWF emphasize investment planning, corporate partnership, and public awareness and action. In the area of coastal resilience, the partnership is looking at continued opportunities for awareness raising and capacity building, and to identify common goals to connect on wetlands, mangroves, and coral reefs in Indonesia, Pakistan, and the Pacific. In the blue economy, focus is on rolling out and using the ADB implementation framework to ensure financing of some of the emerging priorities and promoting the Sustainable Blue Economy Finance Principles. For example, a series of Ocean Policy opinion pieces, co-authored by Ingrid van Wees, ADB vice-president (Finance and Risk Management), and John Tanzer, WWF oceans practice leader, were placed in regional media outlets, targeting countries that are members of the High-Level Panel for a Sustainable Ocean Economy. The collaboration is also engaging with the Association of Southeast Asian Nations Catalytic Green Finance Facility, with promising work on the development of a marine financing facility in Cambodia and Indonesia.

Addressing the illegal wildlife trade. Another impactful area of capacity building was addressing the illegal wildlife trade. The WWF and the Association of Certified Anti-Money Laundering Specialists provided lectures for ADB and partnered on the development of a global free training course that was launched in October 2020. ADB's Trade and Supply Chain Finance Program rolled out this free training certificate in early 2021. Both partners will have an opportunity to showcase areas of cooperation at major events in 2021, including the United Nations Food Systems Summit, the Convention on Biodiversity Conference (COP15), and the United Nations Climate Change Conference (COP26).

Partnership with Plan International. ADB and Plan International reached the end of their second partnership Memorandum of Understanding 2017–2020, following a first partnership in 2013–2016. The partners plan to renew their partnership in 2021. Plan International has supported the NGOC and the YFA since the beginning of its relationship in mobilizing young people from diverse backgrounds to participate in events, knowledge generation, and project activities on meaningful youth engagement in ADB's work. Plan International used its expertise in youth employment to provide much of the content for the APYS, including speakers and facilitators. Plan International provided ADB with youth safeguarding advice and support, managing and mitigating the risks of online harm to young people, which are extensively documented in the media and academic literature. It designed and rolled out e-learning courses in the technical content of the APYS to support youth capacity building and provided a safe online networking forum for participants. In addition, Plan International is providing technical support to the YFA activities for gender mainstreaming and safeguarding, and youth economic empowerment.

Plan International continues to place a secondee in ADB's NGOC. This expertise supported the NGOC and the cohort of youth project designers working on effective youth-led components of projects, including TA projects, and policy initiatives as well as on financing, strategy development, M&E, and the thematic priorities of health and wellness, climate change, and environmental sustainability.

Graduation Approach

The graduation approach, an example of how civil society is developing innovative models to poverty reduction, is a holistic and empirically proven way to address poverty and reduce inequality, a key operational priority of ADB Strategy 2030. BRAC, one of the world's largest NGOs, developed the model in 2002 in Bangladesh. Graduation programs build on targeted social assistance (cash transfers) with livelihoods promotion, delivering a productive asset and technical training, financial inclusion, social empowerment, and coaching and mentoring. Supported by a growing body of global evidence, this comprehensive set of interventions is also referred to as economic inclusion or cash plus programming. Time-bound and carefully sequenced for maximum impact, the interventions give poor and vulnerable households a big push, build their confidence, and sustainably lift them out of the poverty trap. ADB is applying the approach to social protection operations and exploring its suitability for improving livelihood restoration in the context of involuntary resettlement.

In 2020, ADB successfully completed its first graduation pilot in the Philippines and initiated new graduation programs in the country, as well as in India by working with World Vision-India, and in Mongolia. This initiative produced a series of knowledge products, including policy briefs and blog posts for the international community, and an ADB intranet site, which provides resources for ADB staff wanting to learn more about the graduation approach.

Fostering Inclusion of Sexual and Gender Minorities

The International Day Against Homophobia, Transphobia and Biphobia (IDAHOTB) is commemorated every 17 May on the anniversary of the declassification of same-sex attraction as a mental disorder by the World Health Organization in 1990. The IDAHOTB commemorates all incidences of violence and discrimination against any person based on their sexual orientation and gender identity, whether perpetrated by governments or individuals. Following a successful event in 2019, co-organized by the NGOC and the Gender Thematic Group, ADB (through the NGOC) held an event in 2020, in partnership with the World Bank, who then organized a weeklong series of virtual events in conjunction with the European Bank for Reconstruction and Development (EBRD) and the Inter-American Development Bank (IDB).

The ADB-led event focused on "Bridging the LGBTI (lesbian, gay, bisexual, transgender and intersex) data gap," complementing the World Bank and the EBRD event on "Cost of Exclusion" and the IDB event on "Policies for Inclusion." Over 400 ADB staff, civil society representatives, policy makers, and academics attended the ADB event. The panel discussion at ADB's event featured academics from within the Asia and Pacific region, who have conducted important research on the factors that limit the relevance and usability of existing data on the LGBTQI+ (lesbian, gay, bisexual, transgender, queer, intersex, and more) populations in the region, and in the private sector's role in fostering inclusion. Also on the panel were civil society representatives who led grassroots activities with "invisible" LGBTQI+ populations in remote locations, and included representation of lesbian, bisexual and transgender women—groups which can be overlooked through a patriarchal mindset, even within the field of sexual orientation and gender identity. The discussion highlighted important ideas on how to make data collection accessible through use of simpler language and nonthreatening channels of communication.

International Day Against Homophobia, Transphobia and Biphobia online event. ADB organized an online event in May 2020, which tackled issues such as bridging the LGBTI data gap, understanding the cost of exclusion, and promoting policies for inclusion (photo by NGO and Civil Society Center).

VI. WAYS FORWARD

ADB's planned operations in 2020 may have been disrupted by the emergence of the COVID-19 pandemic. Nevertheless, the bank continued to be flexible and agile in delivering its COVID-19 response support to DMCs and in pursuing its Strategy 2030 objectives.[27] More important than the volume of projects, ADB operations teams will focus on project quality with enhanced design and implementation. The change in indicator for CSO engagement, as accounted in ADB's corporate development effectiveness review, is a step toward this direction. ADB is starting to look more closely on the level and quality of civil society participation in its operations and will now account only for what it considers as meaningful CSO engagement as part of its corporate performance. The NGOC also brings in an intern in 2021 to join its team to provide a deeper analysis of the trends in civil society engagement. With the new indicator for measuring the level and quality of its engagement with CSOs, ADB's project teams will be more nuanced in their project design, implementation, and review processes.

In terms of engaging CSOs in its operations and policy review processes, ADB has quickly adapted by shifting to online modes of training and consultations. Its Safeguard Policy Statement, Energy Policy Statement, and Disaster and Emergency Assistance Policy, including its approaches for supporting FCAS, are being prepared by consulting extensively with CSOs in the region. This has allowed ADB to reach more and even new organizations that would have otherwise been unable to participate in its in-person meetings or processes. Guided by ADB's Strategy 2030 and the increased digitalization and widening of direct access to citizens through the internet, ADB will continue to expand its approaches to citizens engagement, including through the Youth for Asia initiative. ADB operations teams have also been more flexible in their contracting arrangements with service delivery organizations to help ease the interruptions brought by the pandemic.

ADB will further seek CSO involvement as it works toward a resilient, inclusive, and green recovery from the impacts of the pandemic. As the bank continues to use the remaining resources for its comprehensive package on the COVID-19 Active Response and Expenditure Program for its DMCs, it will keep on engaging key stakeholders, including CSOs, who sit in committees that provide oversight on the implementation of the program (footnote 27). Furthermore, ADB's TA project,

---

[27] ADB (OPR). 2021. Planning Directions for 2021 and Preparations of Work Program and Budget Framework, 2022–2024. 22 February.

Mitigating the Impacts of COVID-19 through Community-Led Interventions, will capture knowledge of CSO approaches to reaching the most vulnerable populations and of the communities' coping mechanisms to the impacts of the pandemic. ADB will explore potential roles for CSOs in its new $9 billion vaccine initiative called the Asia Pacific Vaccine Access Facility, which provides quick and equitable financing for vaccine procurement to its DMCs.[28] ADB sees CSOs supporting their national and local government health systems on information and awareness raising on the vaccination program, identifying priority populations, and addressing vaccine hesitancy. In all these initiatives, ADB will continue closing the gender gap in the region and will increase CSO involvement in this particular work.

ADB will also explore documenting knowledge on CSO approaches toward increasing public accountability and good governance, particularly on responding to the impacts of the pandemic. It will also showcase CSO innovations in development through the graduation approach knowledge event. At the 54th ADB Annual Meeting of the Board of Governors to be held online, the Civil Society Program will feature CSO initiatives and recommendations to ADB and governments on ensuring equitable COVID-19 response programs, meeting global climate change commitments, and renewing the earnest pursuit of SDGs targets.

As part of aligning its strategies along the global commitments on climate change, ADB pledges to deliver $80 billion in climate finance from 2019 to 2030 and to ensure that 75% of its projects will address climate change mitigation and adaptation by 2030.[29] ADB will listen and collaborate more with various stakeholders, including CSOs, in supporting its DMCs on their own climate commitments and integrating climate considerations in its projects.

Guided by its Strategy 2030 and moving toward a green, resilient, and inclusive recovery through the preceding actions from 2021 onward, ADB will take advantage of maximizing CSO contributions to reaching its development targets and creating greater impact toward a prosperous, inclusive, resilient, and sustainable Asia and the Pacific.

[28]   ADB. 2020. *ADB's Support to Enhance COVID-19 Vaccine Access.* Manila.
[29]   ADB. 2021. Climate Finance in 2020. Infographic. 5 February.

www.ingramcontent.com/pod-product-compliance
Lightning Source LLC
Chambersburg PA
CBHW050057220326
41599CB00045B/7442